The World's
Stupidest
CRIMINALS

The World's
Stupidest
CRIMINALS

Rhian McKay

Michael O'Mara Humour

First published in Great Britain in 2002 by
Michael O'Mara Books Limited
9 Lion Yard
Tremadoc Road
London SW4 7NQ

A CIP catalogue record for this book is available
from the British Library

ISBN (10-digit): 1-84317-171-6
ISBN (13-digit): 978-1-84317-171-3

10 9 8 7 6 5

Designed and typeset by Design 23

www.mombooks.com

Printed and bound in Great Britain by Cox & Wyman,
Reading, Berks

Contents

Introduction

Films, books and the media can sometimes lead us to believe that the world is populated with criminals capable of devising the most Machiavellian of capers and executing them with flawless skill. If you believed everything you heard, you'd think all criminals were geniuses. However, as illustrated by this collection of tales about the ill luck, bad timing, and downright stupidity of the average felon – whether a robber, thief, kidnapper, drink driver or drug dealer – this is very far from being the case!

There have been few of us who, in our time, haven't been tempted by the prospect of making a fast buck, no matter how illegal the method might be. As the following stories demonstrate, however, it doesn't matter how prepared, how organized and how determined you are, something will always go wrong. And when the basic stupidity of your average offender is added into the mix, more often than not you have a recipe for complete disaster! As the stories brought together into this hilarious collection illustrate, crime really doesn't pay!

The Stupidest Disguised CRIMINALS

Obviously, anonymity is the key when it comes to pulling off a successful robbery. There's nothing worse than making off with enough money to set you up in the lap of luxury for life, just to return home to find the police camped out on your doorstep because someone happened to recognize you. The measures the following criminals took to avoid being recognized, however, were perhaps not the most effective…

Eye Can't See You

A man planning to rob a bank in the Ukraine had heard that the best way to hide your identity was to put a bag over your head. He therefore drove to the bank and pulled on a paper bag before bursting through the doors and demanding all the money in the till. He didn't get much further than that, though – he had forgotten to put eye holes in the bag!

Plastic Is Not Fantastic

Another would-be robber, this time in Illinois, had also heard about the bag-over-the-head idea but again came unstuck when it came to the details. He used a plastic bag to disguise himself during his robbery! Halfway through holding up a liquor store he began to suffocate and had to whip off the bag and make a run for it!

Poor Criminal

A man who did not have enough money to buy a proper mask used shaving cream to mask his features during his hold-up. Having smeared his face with the foam, he went into a bank and demanded all the money. On his way out, however, he tripped over and fell flat on his face, and half the shaving cream rubbed off on the carpet, rendering his face almost entirely visible. Though he picked himself up and made a run for it, he was easily traceable with the aid of security videotape and eyewitness descriptions.

On The Run

A thief on the run after holding up a bank ran into a city park to escape his pursuers. He joined in with a group of people out exercising in the park, trying to blend in. He had chosen the wrong group of runners, however – they were a unit of police trainees out for an afternoon jog!

Armoured Thief

A man planning to rob his neighbour's house in the dead of the night bought a suit of armour, reasoning that should he be discovered during the robbery the suit would not only disguise his features, but also help to protect him from any attack. Although the house was only two streets away, it took him over half an hour to walk there in his unwieldy suit and he was spotted by several passersby, who were startled by the strange armoured apparition wandering around the suburban streets. He managed to make it to the house and pick the lock to get in, but once inside, the clanking of his armour immediately woke up the owners. They came downstairs and cornered him, eventually pushing a book case on to him and trapping him. Worse was to come, for the book case squashed his armour so badly that he was unable to get out of it, and he had to spend his first night in police cells in the uncomfortable armour. As the next day was a Sunday, it was two days until a locksmith could be found to cut him free.

Gentleman Thief

A young bank robber had better manners than the average criminal. Instead of barging his way in front of all the other customers to make his hold-up demands, he waited patiently in the queue to be served. He came unstuck, however, when he donned his balaclava while in the line so as to be ready when his turn came. The alarm was raised before he managed to even get to the counter!

Fashion Victim

A man in Spain was arrested under suspicion of having perpetrated a series of bag-snatching offences. He vehemently protested his innocence throughout his arrest. Police were then understandably surprised when he appeared in court wearing an expensive suit which one of the victims identified as having been in the bag he had stolen!

What A Drag!

A man who held up a liquor store chose the unusual disguise of a skimpy green dress and a pink wig. The outfit failed to disguise his tattoos or beard, though, and when police watched the CCTV tape afterwards, they had no problem identifying him as a thief they had previously arrested for other crimes!

The Stupidest
Forgetful
CRIMINALS

When it comes to leaving clues as to their identity, stupid criminals can get even the most basic things wrong. Some of the things left behind by these crooks gave the police officers whose job it was to track them down far too easy a time of it. It just goes to show that criminals can all too often be their own worst enemies.

I Knew I Forgot Something

One forgetful thief, having robbed a liquor store, was very pleased with himself for getting away with a sizeable sum of money, as well as a bonus of a couple of bottles of brandy. He wasn't so pleased later that day, however, when the police caught up with him. They explained that they had been able to track him down with the greatest ease because he had left behind his wallet at the store, complete with credit card and driver's licence!

Schooled In Crime

A man in Kentucky held up a liquor store at gunpoint. The assistant complied with his demands for money, but when the man turned to go she noticed that the man was wearing his high school jacket. The jacket had both his name and the year that he graduated written on the back! Armed with this information, the police had no problem tracking him down and recovering the stolen money.

Laundered Money

One criminal in Louisiana was tracked down in one of the most unconventional ways imaginable. A couple of days after having held up a bank, he took all his shirts to the laundry as usual. The assistant went through his pockets to make sure there was nothing valuable in them, as she did with all the clothes she washed. As well as a little loose change, she was surprised to find a ransom note written on the back of a bank slip. Thinking it was probably a joke, she nevertheless called the police, who were able to identify the note as the one used by the perpetrator of a recent bank robbery. When the man returned to collect his washing, they were waiting to arrest him.

You Lose

Two teenagers were in the process of robbing a convenience store when one spotted a handful of leaflets to enter a competition to win a holiday. While his accomplice was bagging up the money, he filled in one of the leaflets with his name, address and telephone number and dropped it in the box on the counter. The assistant noticed this and pointed out the competition entry to the police when they arrived to investigate. By the time the two boys returned home, the police were already there waiting for them.

Uniformly Stupid

Two cashiers at a large, well-known drug store in Germany decided to rob a post office during their lunch hour. Believing that they had got away with it, the pair were amazed when the police turned up at their place of work to arrest them. Each suspected the other of having confessed to the crime. The arresting officer explained that the answer was a little more obvious – they had not only been wearing their drug store uniforms during the hold up, but had also left their name badges on!

Say Cheese!

A middle-aged woman was having her photograph taken in a photo booth at a railway station in Manchester. Just at the moment that the photograph was being taken by the machine, a thief leaned in and grabbed her handbag. When the picture was developed the woman saw that there was a clear shot of his head behind her, which the police were able to use to identify and arrest the bag snatcher.

Would You Credit It?

An expert lock picker in Italy who had used his credit card to jimmy open locked doors and thus break into many homes in the area was finally caught when he forgot to pick up the card, having put it down in one of the houses he had burgled.

Spell Check

A young woman arrested in Australia for a traffic offence tried to outwit the police officer by giving him a false name. Not only did she overlook the fact that he had her car registration details and could easily cross reference them against the name she had provided, she also had problems spelling the alias she had chosen!

Size Is Important!

A seven-foot-tall man living in a small village in Wales walked into the post office and demanded all the money in the safe. The village was small enough for all of the inhabitants to know each other, at least by sight, and the man's stature made him particularly noticeable. The paper bag he wore over his head while robbing the post office did little to render him unrecognizable – especially since the assistant he held up was his next-door neighbour!

The Stupidest Slow CRIMINALS

Returning to the scene of a crime is a text-book error but one which our stupid criminals seem all too happy to make, over and over and over again. Some criminals are so hopeless at making a quick getaway from the scene of their crime that they don't even get as far as leaving it!

Don't Forget Your Shopping List

A gang of teenagers in Brazil were on a beach holiday for a week but, barely three days in, they had run out of money. Unwilling to cut their holiday short and return home so soon, they decided that the best solution was to hold up a local supermarket. They stole a variety of items to see them through the rest of the week – bread, milk, biscuits, chocolate and some cash. As soon as they had fled, the store manager called the police, who arrived promptly. Promptly enough, in fact, to arrest the group! After realizing that they had forgotten to steal one more item – butter – the forgetful teenagers had returned to the store barely five minutes later to do so!

No Complaints Please!

A gang of men held up a pizza take-away late one night, not only making off with the cash but also stealing a large pizza which was sitting on the counter ready to be picked up by a customer. As soon as they left, the manager called the police. He was just in the process of explaining what had happened when he was amazed to see the gang return. They had returned to complain that the pizza they had stolen was burnt! They were promptly arrested.

A Cycle Of Errors

A man in Montreal was apprehended after a series of mishaps that occurred when he tried to hold up a drive-through restaurant. His first, rather basic, mistake was to ride a bicycle through the drive-through, thus drawing considerable attention to himself. He then demanded money with a gun that was very clearly made out of plastic – it was green! Nevertheless, the intimidated cashier, perhaps doubting his sanity by this stage, handed over the money.

When the time came to make his getaway, the hapless thief discovered that he had yet another problem to contend with – a flat tyre. By this point the cashier had pushed the security button to alert the police, who arrived in plenty of time to apprehend the inept cyclist who was still attempting to mend his puncture outside the booth!

Not Your Average Start To The Day

A Californian man broke into a convenience store in the dead of night, intending to rob the safe. He decided the best way into the building was to lower himself in via the skylight, which would take him straight into

the back office. Being a bit overweight, however, he realized that he couldn't quite squeeze through the narrow gap. Thinking that he could make it through if he removed his thick trousers and underwear, he dropped them through the window and attempted to follow them. Removing his clothes had not done the trick, however, and the unlucky thief became stuck! He had to stay there all night until the cleaner came into the office first thing in the morning and looked up to find his naked bottom half dangling from the ceiling.

Crime Is Such Hard Work

Having broken into a house, a robber in New Zealand was loading up his car with the various valuables he had found. The last item on his list of things to steal was the television, which was very big and heavy. He turned it on to check that it worked, not wanting to make an unnecessary trip if it didn't. His favourite programme was just starting, and, safe in the knowledge that the owners would be away for some hours yet, he settled down on the sofa to watch it. However, tired after all that carrying and lifting, he soon fell asleep and began to snore away in front of the television. He was still sleeping like a baby when the owners returned from their night out and found him there!

Falling At The Last Hurdle

Police were baffled when they were called to the scene of a recent bank robbery in New Zealand. The criminal had worn a mask and had left no clues whatsoever as to his identity. The police had all but given up hope of ever locating the money when, a week later, they were presented with a rather large clue. The perpetrator walked back into the same bank and tried to pay all the money, a very large sum, into the account that he held there.

The Stupidest Greedy CRIMINALS

Sometimes, petty crime doesn't yield enough to satisfy some miscreants. All criminals dream of that job that will set them, and their loved ones, up for life. Such a job is remarkably hard to come by but it doesn't stop many stupid criminals from hoping. The following wrongdoers got just a little bit too greedy and paid the price accordingly …

In For A Penny, In For A Pound

A man in Inverness burst into a post office and took four very full bags of money. Delighted with his loot, he made his escape on foot. However, each of the bags contained only pennies and were extremely heavy. The man was easily caught by the police as he staggered very slowly down the pavement!

A Hard-Working Criminal

A man in Chicago held up a convenience store, demanding all the money in the till. However, as it was still early in the morning there was not much cash in it. Deciding it was not enough, the robber tied up the clerk, donned his uniform and worked the till for two hours until the police eventually showed up and arrested him!

In The Bag?

A man who snatched a bag from a woman out walking her dog in the park was most disgusted to open it up at home and find it was the contents of her pooper scooper!

Keep It In The Family

A middle-aged woman was arrested in Canada on three counts of arson. She explained that she had been setting the fires in order to assist her son in his career. He had recently enrolled in the local fire department!

You've Got To Hand It To Them

A woman in Texas became fed up with her boyfriend playing games on the computer she had bought him for his birthday. He played at all hours of the day and night and would go for weeks barely speaking to her because he was so intent on the screen. Eventually, she reached the end of her tether and decided to take radical action to get her boyfriend's attention. Her best friend had mentioned that there was a group of boys who were frequently in trouble with the police and who sometimes hung out around the end of her street. The woman approached them one day and offered them money to break into her house and to steal the computer, an offer they jumped at. She told them when she and her boyfriend would be out of the house, the best way to break in, and where the computer could be found.

All did not go to plan, however. When the couple returned home on the evening she had told the gang to do the break-in, she received as great a surprise as her boyfriend. The teenagers had got greedy and not only taken the computer, but a lot of other things as well, including all the woman's jewellery, clothes and shoes!

Short-Changed

A young woman walked into a bookstore in Glasgow and, putting a twenty pound note on the counter, asked for change. When the assistant opened the till she pulled out a knife and demanded all the money in it. The cashier handed over all the money, and the woman made a run for it, leaving the twenty pound note on the desk. When the thief got home and counted the money she was dismayed to realize that the money in the till came to barely sixteen pounds. She had left the bookstore with a small profit from the incident!

Game On!

A house in Kentucky was broken into while the owners were out for the day. As soon as they discovered the crime the family called the police. The thief's haul included money, expensive clothes, jewellery and the tickets to an upcoming baseball game. On the off-chance that he would be a big enough fan of the sport (and a big enough fool) to turn up there, the investigating police officers went to the game the following weekend. Sure enough, they found the man not only sitting in his neighbour's seat, but also wearing his clothes and jewellery!

Counsel For The Defence

Two men were arrested on four counts of armed robbery. At their trial, they explained that they had been trying to raise money to fund themselves through law school!

Snakes Alive!

A man who picked up an unattended briefcase from a train station got a lot more than he bargained for. When he opened it at home he was shocked, and not a little scared, to find it contained not money or valuables, but a small and deadly adder. The owner of the case had been transporting it to a zoo in another state – he said that the thief was extremely lucky not to have been bitten by the lethal snake.

Dead Pleased

A fifty-year-old house robber from Perth was delighted with his good luck when one night he broke into a house to find a very valuable collection of rare books. He spent some time carrying the heavy books out to his car before driving away, very pleased with his spoils. Sweating from the exercise and the fear of being discovered, he should have called it a day, but, instead, he decided to pull another job that night. Unfortunately, by this stage he was so exhausted by all the carrying that he had a heart attack and keeled over while in the process of robbing the next house. The owner of the house returned at midnight to find him sprawled out on the carpet, dead.

The Stupidest
Big-Mouthed
CRIMINALS

Getting caught is an eventuality
every criminal should consider,
especially the stupid ones! Whether
it's saying too much or not saying
enough, some foolish felons really
should have spent some time
getting their stories straight
beforehand …

Make Your Mind Up

A man in Belgium, having being charged with robbing a jewellery store in Liege, came up with a novel defence. After giving several alibis, all of which were easily exposed by the police to be lies, he finally admitted that he couldn't have committed the crime they were accusing him of as he was breaking into a school at the time. The police then not only arrested him for breaking into the school, but also for the additional crime of wasting police time!

Which Crime?

A man from a small town near Swansea was stopped on the street by the police in a routine stop-and-search exercise. Finding a lot of money on his person, they questioned him about it, suspecting that it could be linked to the bank robbery that had taken place in the town the previous day. Obviously not the quickest thinker in the world, the man told them that the money had nothing to do with the robbery, but that he was a drug dealer, and the money was the proceeds from his business. When the police replied that if it was drug money they would have to confiscate it, the man blurted out, 'No, no, you can't take it. It didn't all come from the bank robbery, at least fifty pounds of it's mine, fair and square!' – thus dropping himself right in it!

No Surrender

A man in Brazil who had terrorized his neighbours with a gun retreated to his own house. When the police arrived he refused to come out, threatening to shoot any officer who came near. The police evacuated the immediate area and laid siege to the building. It was several hours before one of the officers noticed that the man had somehow escaped and was standing behind the police barricades shouting, 'Come out with your hands up!' at the empty house!

Say Again?

A man suspected of mugging an old lady was put in a ID parade so that the victim could identify him. When the detective in charge of the line-up told each of the men to say in turn the words 'Give me your money or I'll blow your f***ing head off!', the robber shouted out indignantly: 'That's not what I said, I said "blow your damn head off!"'

Holy Cow!

A supermarket security guard spotted a woman stuffing a large leg of frozen beef inside her coat. When he confronted her as she attempted to leave the store, she adopted a surprised look and claimed the beef had fallen from above and landed inside her coat. She stuck to this rather dubious story even at her trial!

Tongue-Tied

A woman in Oklahoma burst into a post office planning to frighten staff and customers into submission by screaming 'Put your f***ing hands up, this is a stick-up!' However, her nerves got the better of her, and she said instead, 'Put your sticky hands up, this is a f*** up!' After a brief pause, everyone in the post office began to laugh and, embarrassed, the woman fled the place empty-handed.

Honesty Is Not Always The Best Policy

A young woman on a moving train had her bag snatched by a thief. The thief had nowhere to run to, however, and he was soon cornered by a train guard who told him he was going to be taken back to the woman for a positive identification. Misunderstanding his comment somewhat, as soon as the robber saw the woman he told the guard: 'Yes, officer, that is the woman I robbed.'

Makeshift Lie-Detector

A man living in a small town in Texas who was well-known to the police as a criminal had nevertheless managed to get away with committing various petty misdemeanours for several years, due to a lack of evidence. Two policemen who had been following his criminal career for a while eventually got fed up and decided to arrest him anyway.

They told him he would have to face a lie-detector test at the police station in order to help them prove whether he was guilty or not. It being a small and badly equipped police station, they did not have a lie-detector machine to hand, but they decided not to let that bother them!

They placed a colander on the man's head and used a piece of wire string which they pretended was plugged into the photocopier. They then questioned the man about the various crimes they suspected him of perpetrating, and every time he said something they thought to be false, one of them pressed the 'copy' button on the photocopier so that it spat out a copy of a piece of paper on which they had printed

'HE'S LYING'. After half an hour or so of what the man clearly believed to be an effective and impressively high-tech interrogation, he thought the game was up, and confessed comprehensively to all the crimes they suspected him of – as well as a few they didn't!

Catch Me If You Can

In a textbook example of pride going before a fall, it was the ego of the perpetrator of a successful series of bank robberies that managed to land him in prison. After watching countless news stories reporting how baffled the police were by the identity of the robber, he called a local police station to brag that they would never catch him. He went on at some length about his finely developed criminal skills, and his experience in evading detection. His boasts were somewhat undermined, however, by the fact that he forgot to block his number, which the police were easily able to trace and use to track him down. When they caught up with him a few hours later, he was on the telephone to another police station, making yet more proud boasts!

So Sue Me!

After the robbery of a petrol station, in which the cashier was viciously beaten, the local paper ran a story detailing the crime, and describing the perpetrator as a 'particularly hardened and unpleasant individual, posing a serious threat to society'. The detectives investigating the robbery, who, up till that point, had few leads to assist them, were amazed when one of their uniformed colleagues was stopped in the street the next day by the robber. He showed the policewoman the article, complained indignantly about its depiction of him, and asked if she thought that he had grounds for suing for libel!

Putting The Boot In

A patrol officer who pulled over a man speeding on the motorway was about to issue a standard fine when the man suddenly blurted out, 'You're not going to check in the boot, are you?' The officer, who up till then had no intention of doing so, opened the boot of the car to find several pounds of marijuana inside, which the man had been taking to sell in another city.

The Stupidest
Misdirected
CRIMINALS

The golden rule when it comes to property is said to be location, location, location. This rule could also be applied to crime, as the following stupid criminals learned, much to their cost ...

Neighbourhood Watch

A young man from Nottingham made a rather elementary mistake when he chose to rob a newsagent. Almost as soon as he pulled out his gun, several policemen seemed suddenly to appear out of nowhere, forcing him to surrender. It was later explained to him that he had perhaps made a serious error when he decided to hold up a newsagent situated directly across the street from the local police station!

Out Of The Frying Pan And Into The Fire

A young man on the run from the police after having held up a bank scrambled over a high barbed-wire fence in his desperation to escape from his pursuers. What he hadn't realized was that this was the outer fence of the local prison! The police on his trail did not bother pursuing him any further – they merely called the prison and asked them to apprehend him.

It's All In The Details

A man in Detroit had spent months meticulously planning a bank robbery. When the day of the heist came, he burst through the doors and told everyone to get on the floor. The one flaw in the excecution of his plan was that, instead of the bank, he had accidentally entered the police station next door!

Vaulty Sense of Direction

Three Swiss criminals hit upon the idea of breaking into the vault of a bank via the walls of an adjoining building. Having rented the building, spent a fortune on drilling machinery, and spent hours gradually breaking through walls so as not to alert anyone, they finally made it through only to discover that they had misjudged the location of the vault. They had actually been drilling through the walls of the ladies' toilets!

Highly Unconventional

A pair of bag snatchers chose the wrong target for their latest job. An international convention was being held in their town, and, thinking that this would provide them with rich pickings, the pair grabbed a bag of jewellery from a street vendor. What they hadn't realized, however, was that the convention was being held for motorcycle policemen. The two criminals had got barely half a mile away before being caught by nearly twenty policemen on motorbikes.

It's Snow Joke

A female house-breaker in France thought that she had found the perfect house to rob with impunity. Located in a remote part of Brittany, the house was very isolated and she knew that, as the owners were away, she could afford to take her time. She should have checked the weather forecast beforehand, however, because, in a chronic piece of bad timing, it started to snow heavily while she was robbing the house. When the owners returned two days later and called the police, the officers were able to see her footprints quite clearly in the snow and track them all the way back to her house!

No Way Out

Having heard from an ex-employee that the takings were often left there overnight, a man decided to rob a local restaurant in the dead of night. He entered the building through the chimney but, having collected the loot, realized it would be impossible to leave via this route. All the doors were locked, with no sign of the keys, and when he tried to break the windows, he discovered that the glass was shatterproof. With no other exit he had no option but to call the police to let him out.

Robber Without A Clue

Having just mugged a couple of young boys in a side street in Wisconsin, a man was on the run from the angry father of one of them. He dived into the boot of an unattended car to hide. On reflection, he realized he had not chosen the best place to hide, for not only had he overlooked the fact that the boot would lock automatically once he had pulled the door down on himself, he also had the bad luck to have chosen a car belonging to an undercover police officer, as evidenced by the spare uniform kept in there. He kept quiet for a while, scared of being caught, but at the end of the second day the policeman was alerted by the noise of sobs coming from the boot of his car. He opened it up to find one very bedraggled, thirsty and hungry mugger, and arrested him on the spot!

The Stupidest
Easily
Foiled
CRIMINALS

Police officers are not the only
people who manage
successfully to foil crime.
Sometimes the stupid criminal's
worst enemy can be the man –
or woman – in the street ...

Love On The Run

An amorous criminal from Bolivia was making his getaway after a successful robbery at a hardware store, when he spotted an attractive woman on the pavement. Very struck with her good looks, he stopped to chat with her and asked her for a date, scribbling his name and phone number down. Later, watching the television, the woman saw the CCTV tape on the local news and recognized the man robbing the hardware store as the same one who had propositioned her. Being a responsible citizen, and not as taken with the man as he was with her, she called the police who were able to track him down using the name and phone number she had for him.

Faking It

A housewife in South Carolina came up with a scam to supplement her husband's earnings. She printed counterfeit money, paying it into her bank account then transferring it into that of her husband. It worked beautifully for several months – they were able to buy a new house with a pool, a new car and afford exotic holidays – until one day she got a little too greedy and tried to pay in a particularly large denomination note into her account. The bank teller didn't have to be particularly observant to notice the counterfeit – it was a million dollar note!

Queue-cumber Jumper

A teenager in the process of robbing a grocery store in Missouri was unexpectedly foiled by a very impatient customer. Furious that the robber had jumped the queue when she had been waiting for several minutes to be served, the irate middle-aged woman grabbed a cucumber and hit him on the head with it. The robber was momentarily stunned by the blow, allowing the storekeeper enough time to tie him up and prevent him escaping until the police arrived.

Honour Among Thieves

Three would-be bank robbers spent all Sunday night waiting patiently in a London bank after attacking a cleaner and forcing their way inside. When the cashier arrived in the morning, they leapt on her and ordered her to open up the vault. She told them she could not open it by herself – it needed two employees to unlock it – but that she had seen the bank manager having a cigarette outside. She helpfully volunteered to go and fetch him if they would let her go for a minute. The trio trustingly agreed to this, and let her out, whereupon she went straight to a phone box to summon the police. The trio were still patiently waiting for the cashier's return when the police burst in to arrest them.

Young Guns

A pair of teenagers broke into a neighbour's house, intending to rob it. Finding the owner in the house, they seized him and bundled him into a cupboard under the stairs. This was where the man kept his guns, however, and the two wannabe robbers found themselves waking up in hospital shortly afterwards!

Doing Your Duty

A man in a small town who was wanted for several minor misdemeanours, such as traffic violations and shoplifting, had successfully evaded arrest for several months. Every time the police came round to his house to arrest him, he would lock himself in and declare that he would shoot anyone who tried to enter. Deciding the man was not really worth the risk of bloodshed, every time this happened the police officers decided to leave him to it.

One day a letter asking him to present himself at the local court to do jury service was delivered to the man. He turned up at court on the stated date, whereupon he was recognized by a couple of police officers who were there in connection with another case, and finally arrested!

Identified As A Failed Bank Robber

An intelligent young bank worker was approached by a man who told her he was holding up the bank, and demanded that she give him all the money. Sizing the man up, the cashier decided he was a little slow and that she could easily put him off. She told him that he needed an identity card in order to rob the bank. Disappointed as he didn't have his with him, the man turned around and left empty-handed!

The Stupidest Clumsy CRIMINALS

Sometimes, a life of crime definitely isn't all it's cracked up to be. What with the irregular hours, the stress and all the tearing about it can all prove too much for some crooks. Crime, as the following mishaps demonstrate, can be a dangerous, even lethal, business where the following clumsy crooks are concerned.

Falling At The First Hurdle

Despite having meticulously planned his hold up and getaway beforehand, a Belgian would-be bank robber fell at the first hurdle, quite literally. He tripped up on the steps on his way into the bank. The fall dislodged his mask and caused him to slide across the floor towards the cashier's desk. Picking himself up, the concussed man fell forward across the counter, brandished his gun and declared: 'This is a sit-up!'

Fat Chance!

After holding up a bank, an overweight bank robber made a dash for the door carrying his bag of loot. Thinking that the automatic doors would have been locked as soon as the cashier pressed the alert button, he headed instead for the revolving doors in order to make his escape. Unfortunately, he was a little too plump to get through safely and he got stuck. The police had to call the fire brigade to cut him loose!

Don't Leave It Till The Last Minute

Sometimes, forward planning does no good at all. Thinking that the best time to rob a store would be just as it was shutting for the day, because then the tills would be at their fullest and there would be no customers around to hinder him, a man raced into a department store in Leicester just before it closed. Having stolen the day's takings from the nearest cashier, he then raced back towards the automatic doors in order to make his escape. In a chronic case of bad timing, however, the doors had just been locked, and the man knocked himself out by running headfirst into them! The store's security guard had to pick him up from the floor to arrest him.

Caught With Your Trousers Down

Police finally caught up with a thief running away from the scene of a bank robbery when his low slung trousers fell down and tripped him up. Asking the officers to give him a minute to pull his trousers up, he then made another dash for it, before being brought up short when they fell down once again!

Handed Them On A Plate

A man in Norway attempted to pull a cash machine off the wall by attaching it to a chain tied to the back of his van.

Unfortunately for him, the chain merely pulled the van's bumper off. Panicked, the man quickly drove off, forgetting that his number plate was on the bumper still attached to the machine. The police traced the number plate and arrested him the following day.

Keep The Noise Down

Another pair of criminals had a little more success when they too decided to pull a cash machine off the wall. This time they actually managed to pull it free. The high speed at which they drove off, however, not only made a loud noise of squealing tyres, but also caused sparks to fly up from the metal of the machine as it was dragged along the tarmac. They attracted the attention of passersby for streets around, as well as the local police!

See the Light

A man paid a high price for trying to rob the safe of a convenience store in the middle of the night, despite – or rather, because of – being better prepared than your average stupid criminal. Knowing it would be dark in the store and he would be unable to switch on the lights, he brought a flashlight along with him. While he was crawling in through the window he had to put the torch between his teeth as he needed both his hands free. Unfortunately, he slipped over and fell face first on to the windowsill – the force rammed the flashlight back into the base of his skull and killed him instantly.

That Fell Flat

A middle-aged man decided to kill his wife by pushing her out of the window of the ninth-storey flat they shared, thinking he could easily explain her death by saying she had fallen out. After pushing her, he looked out of the window and saw to his dismay that she was not quite dead. Impetuously, he decided that the best way to finish her off before she told anyone what he had done was to jump out after her and land on top of her. Unfortunately for him, he missed.

It's A Knock-Out!

A passerby was bemused to find a man lying unconscious on the pavement in the early hours of the morning, a brick lying near his head. Thinking that he had been assaulted, she alerted the police as well as calling an ambulance. The police also thought that he had been hurt and it wasn't until the man came to and sheepishly admitted the truth that they called off their hunt for the attacker. He explained that he had gone to a liquor store to get some vodka, but that it had been shut as it was well after closing time. Desperate for a drink, he had then decided to throw a brick through the window. What he hadn't realized was that the glass was shatterproof – the brick had bounced straight back at him and struck him on the forehead!

Trigger-Happy

A thief running from the scene of his latest post office hold-up in Texas tripped over a loose paving stone and managed accidentally to shoot himself in the thigh! He stumbled on until he found a taxi, but shortly afterwards passed out from the pain. The taxi driver drove him to the nearest hospital where the police duly caught up with him.

Dead Surprised

A thief decided to break into a local restaurant via the air vent on the roof. What he had not realized, however, was that the vent led straight into the restaurant's large oven. When the oven failed to work the next day, the chef called a repairman. He found the man stuck inside the vent, having suffocated to death.

The Stupidest
Accomplice
CRIMINALS

When planning a caper, it helps if you can find an accomplice who you can trust in a tight spot. The following tales are perfect illustrations that, if you're intending to pull off a successful crime, it's vital to pick your friends wisely…

Know Your Enemy

A pair of criminals burst into a bank nervously brandishing shotguns. The first criminal screamed out, 'No one move, or I'll shoot!' All the customers and staff obediently stood stock-still. The second criminal moved towards the counter to start gathering the cash – whereupon his nervous partner shot him!

Leg It!

Bursting out of a bank, having successfully robbed it of a large sum of cash, a robber from Bristol thought he was home and dry. He had arranged for a getaway car, a hiding place for the money and a place to lie low for a while. When he ran out to where he had arranged to meet the driver of his getaway car, however, his accomplice misjudged the stopping distance and ran him over, breaking both his legs.

A Case of Shooting Yourself in the Foot

A man in South Africa enlisted the help of his friend to run an insurance scam. He was heavily insured, and would be due a large payout should he be seriously injured. The deal was that they would split the money between them. Wanting an injury serious enough to merit a payout, but not life-threatening, the man asked his friend to shoot him in the shoulder. Unfortunately, his friend was a chronically bad shot and instead shot him in the chest. The accomplice, panicked and guilt-ridden because he believed the man was dying, confessed their plan to the ambulance men who came to their assistance. The man survived, but both were arrested for conspiracy to defraud.

Double Trouble

Two men who had just been convicted for an attempted armed robbery were being transported together to a prison in another district. Their legs were chained together to ensure that neither one could escape. Halfway through the journey, the van pulled over at a service station and the pair were allowed out to use the bathroom. In a pre-planned move, both the criminals made a sudden dash for freedom together, taking the guards momentarily by surprise. They had got barely fifty yards from the van, however, before they tried to go in different directions. The chain that tied them to each other got caught on a lamp post. Each frantically trying to break free by altering their direction, they succeeded only in wrapping the chain several times round the post. The only problem the guards experienced when recapturing the felons was having to untangle them from each other and from the lamp post!

Double Vision

Two policemen pulled over a car to tell the driver that one of his rear lights was broken. They found a very drunk driver in charge of the vehicle and another, even drunker, man sitting on his lap, facing the wrong way. From their rambling and confused explanations, the officers eventually pieced together what had happened. Realizing that he was very drunk, the first man had asked his companion to swap places with him in the belief that he was less intoxicated. Not only was he wrong in this supposition – they were both very drunk – but they had not thought of stopping the car while they changed seats! They were both arrested.

The Stupidest Car CRIMINALS

Cars are vital to many criminals, allowing them to make a speedy escape from the scene of their latest crime or giving them a relatively easy target to steal. Stupid criminals don't always make the best use of vehicles, however, and can end up in an even worse pickle because of them ...

Criminally Stupid

A man in Cheshire was arrested by a policeman who found him throwing up at a roadside next to a camper van and a puddle of sewage. The man admitted to trying to siphon petrol from the van, but explained that he had accidentally put his hose into the vehicle's sewage tank instead. He had had to put his mouth to the hose to begin the liquid-drawing process, but had been taken aback when it was the contents of the toilet rather than petrol which had come out. This criminal was luckier than most, though, as the owner of the camper van declined to press charges, saying it was the best laugh he had had in ages!

Dead Ringer

A woman in Switzerland had her car stolen from outside her house during the night. While browsing through the second-hand car adverts in the local paper she noticed that there was a car listed which was the same model, colour and year as the one that she had had stolen. Suspicious, she called the phone number listed and arranged to look at the car the next day. She then called the police and asked them to come with her. Sure enough, the car was hers – her sunglasses and jewellery were still in the glove compartment – and the man who met them was arrested immediately.

Nice Plan

A man kidnapped a woman at gun point and forced her to drive to two different cashpoints on opposite sides of town. He withdrew large amounts of cash from his *own* bank accounts and then let her go!

The Evidence Would Suggest Otherwise

A man in Canada had a good night out at the pub with all his friends. Despite having got very drunk during the course of the evening, he decided he would drive the five miles home. On his way, he was stopped by two police officers who noticed his car weaving erratically all over the road. They asked him to get out of his car so that they could administer a breathalyser test. Just as he was about to take the test, the policemen were distracted by something happening a couple of blocks down the street, and the man, seizing the opportunity to make his escape, quickly hopped back in the car and drove off. Somehow he made it home safely, congratulating himself on a close shave.

The next morning, he was awoken by a ring at the doorbell. Very hungover, he made his way downstairs to find the same two officers on his doorstep. They accused him of having being drunk in charge of a vehicle the previous night, which he strenuously denied. His denials were somewhat undermined, however, when the officers opened up his garage and found their patrol car parked inside!

Help Me Out

A man who had just discovered that his brand new car, complete with all the latest gadgets and extras, had been stolen from outside his house, was amazed to receive a call from the car thief. The cheeky thief had found his number in the address book in the glove compartment and was calling on his mobile phone to ask how the complicated car stereo worked! Furious, the man called him a few choice names and then hung up. However, as he did so, he realized that his phone would have stored the caller's number and he immediately rang the police with it. Using the number, the police were easily able to trace the criminal to his home and found the car parked outside.

Safe Stop

Four criminals broke into a bank, intending to steal the contents of the safe in its vault. When they made their way into the vault, however, they found that they were not as skilled at safe-breaking as they had thought. After nearly an hour of attempting to get at the loot inside, they were forced to rethink their plan.

They decided the best option would be to take the safe away with them, so that they could break into it at their leisure, without the fear of being caught at any minute. The safe was securely attached to the floor, however, and even with the four of them pushing, they could not dislodge it. They then decided to run a chain from their

van through the windows and offices of the bank, and attach it to the safe in order to pull it free of its anchorings. This plan worked, and with an almighty wrench, the safe was finally loose, although it caused immense destruction as it was dragged out onto the pavement.

The van sped off at high speed, with the safe still being pulled behind it, and the criminals resumed their debate as to how best to open it when they got to their hideout. They did not get that far, however, as when the driver stopped suddenly at a red light, the safe careered into the back of the van and managed to lodge itself under the bumper, lifting the rear of the vehicle off the ground. The criminals were stuck there until they were spotted by a passing patrol car a few minutes later.

Running On Empty

Three car thieves in Italy decided that there were rich pickings to be had from stealing three cars from a car transporter parked at a motorway service station. Each took a car and drove off. They didn't get very far, though, as the cars had only been filled with one gallon of petrol each! The vehicles were later found abandoned on the hard shoulder only yards away from the service station.

Classy Criminals

A man in Mexico was distraught when the expensive car he had bought just a week earlier was stolen from outside his house. Later that same day, he received a telephone call from an anonymous man demanding eight thousand dollars for the return of the car. The man reluctantly paid the ransom and the next day he woke up to find his car, in perfect condition, parked outside his house. There was a polite note tucked under the windscreen wipers thanking him for the money and assuring him that his car was now 'insured' against theft for the next year.

However, a couple of weeks later, the man woke up and found that his car had again gone missing. Once again, that afternoon, the man received the call asking for the eight thousand dollars ransom money, whereupon the man complained that his car had supposedly been insured against theft. The anonymous caller quickly hung up. The next day, when the man looked outside his front door it was to see his car parked outside. There was a bottle of champagne inside along with a note of apology.

Backseat Driver

One of the most important things to plan for when committing a robbery is the getaway. Having held up a delicatessen, a thief in Cardiff realized that he would not be able to escape quickly enough on foot. He therefore forced a woman who was passing by into a car, demanding that she drive him to safety. However, the woman had never driven a car, let alone got her licence, and was unable even to start the car. When the police arrived, having been called by the manager of the delicatessen, they found the car still parked outside the store. The robber was in the back seat shouting furiously at the hapless woman as she tried yet again to turn the ignition on!

SuperGran

An elderly lady in Brazil had just spent the afternoon visiting her daughter and grandchildren. When she left their house and returned to her car, which was parked on the street, she found three men sitting inside it. Terrified, but determined not to have her car stolen she pulled out her gun and forced the men to get out. When she got into the car she found that her key did not fit the ignition. She looked up the road and saw her car which was actually parked a few feet away – identical to the one the men had been sitting in. Getting into her own car, she drove to the local police station and apologetically reported the incident. The officer at the desk, fighting back laughter, explained that three very pale and frightened men had come in ten minutes earlier and reported an unlikely car hijacking by an elderly lady!

Candid Camera

A man driving into work one morning had not noticed that he was speeding and was very surprised to receive a letter from the police explaining that he had been caught by an automatic speed camera, along with an invoice for twenty pounds and a photograph of his car. Unwilling to believe that he had actually been speeding, he sent back a photograph of a cheque for twenty pounds. A few days later, he received a letter back from the police department containing a photograph of a set of handcuffs!

Underage Driver

A boy of fourteen was arrested while driving through the streets of Philadelphia without a licence. Despite the fact that he had never driven a car before, the boy managed to negotiate his way safely through four miles of heavy traffic, sitting on a cushion to allow him to see over the steering wheel. The boy explained he had learnt his driving skills from computer games!

Tyre-less Car Thief

A woman driving a stolen car had to pull over on the hard shoulder of the motorway when she discovered it had a puncture. Rather than giving it up as a bad job or even trying to change the tyre herself, she flagged down a police car to help. While he was changing the tyre the policeman did a routine security check on the number plate and found out it was stolen. He very chivalrously finished changing the tyre for the benefit of the real owners, before taking the woman in!

How Far To The Nearest Police Station?

A man's car was stolen while he was shopping for his weekly groceries. He was just standing on the kerb, wondering what best to do about it, when the answer came in the most unexpected way. The young man who had stolen the car pulled up in the vehicle and asked him for directions. The man quickly called a passing police officer, who grabbed the miscreant and directed him to the nearest police station!

Gas Attack!

The police were called to the assistance of an armoured lorry which seemed to be in some difficulties. The driver seemed to be signalling for help as he drove down the road, swinging his door open and shut and lurching erratically from left to right. Believing that the truck had perhaps been hijacked, the police gave chase for several miles. When the truck was eventually pulled over, however, the driver explained that he had merely been trying to get some fresh air in after the passenger guard had farted!

Added Extras

A police patrol officer gave chase to a car which had the top half of a lamp post laid across the front bonnet. When he caught up with the driver, who was very drunk, he asked where the lamp post had come from. The driver very patiently explained to the officer that it had come with the car. He stuck to this story even when the policeman took him in for further questioning!

The Stupidest Drunken CRIMINALS

The demon drink has proved to be the undoing of many a stupid criminal. Whether desperate for a drink or dazed and confused because of it, many people have found that 'just the one' ended up landing them behind bars of a very different kind …

Skunk Patrol

Policemen aren't the only ones who help to catch stupid criminals – sometimes Mother Nature lends a hand too. A man from Toronto was on the run from police after a serious assault on a fellow drinker in a local pub. His car ran out of petrol, forcing him to abandon it on the roadside and make a dash into the woods on foot. He was making good speed when he was brought up short by a skunk he tripped over as he plunged headlong through the under-growth. The skunk blasted him full in the face with its scent, rendering the man temporarily dizzy and disorientated. The police were able to catch up with him, but had to hold their noses as they led him back to the car.

Lost Your Bottle?

A man in Minnesota held up a liquor store, demanding all the money in the till. While the cashier was putting the money in a bag the robber asked for a large bottle of whisky from behind the counter. The cashier refused to hand it over as he didn't believe that the man was over twenty-one. The man produced his identification card to prove his age and finally left with the money and the whisky. By the time he got home the police were waiting for him as the cashier had promptly called the police and supplied them with his name and address.

Drunk in Charge

On his way home from work, a man called into his local drinking haunt and had a couple of drinks too many. Despite his friends trying to restrain him as he was well over the limit, he decided to drive home. He was driving fairly well, and was halfway home when the car broke down. He got out of the car and began to push it home, but soon became too tired to continue. He went to a phone box and called the police to help him get home. They arrived shortly afterwards and arrested him for being drunk in charge of a vehicle.

Drunk and Disorganized

A man in Florida was pulled over by the police who had noticed his car weaving and lurching erratically as they passed him on the freeway. Suspecting that he was drunk, they asked him to walk along the straight line on the tarmac, something which the man spectacularly failed to do, weaving and stumbling all over the road. When the police accused him of being drunk the man reacted with indignation and outrage. The reason he could not walk along the straight line, he informed them, was that he had a glass eye. Still suspicious, the police officer asked him which one. The man thought for a while, before eventually answering, 'Both of them.'

Caught Short

A police car on patrol spotted a car lurching erratically over the road. Suspecting the driver was drunk, they pulled the car over. Their suspicions were reinforced when they found the man's speech was slurred and he had difficulty standing up. They asked him to take a breathalyser test but he refused, telling them that he was desperately in need of the bathroom, and that he feared that the strain of blowing into the breathalyser would cause him to have an accident! The patrol officers arrested him for refusing to co-operate.

This time, though, our stupid criminal had the last laugh, for the judge at his trial ruled that he had given a good enough reason to refuse a breathalyser test!

The Stupidest
Courtroom
CRIMINALS

You would think that criminals
would not be keen to advertise
their crimes. Amazingly, some
stupid criminals are so keen on
their rights that they will take legal
action over something that went
wrong during the crime. Even
more amazingly, the courts
occasionally uphold
their claims ...

Court In The Act

A lawyer in Winnipeg who was defending a man on trial for assault was in the middle of an impassioned and eloquent plea for the man's bail to be reduced. He explained that the defendant was a family man with strong ties to the area, who had every intention of seeing the trial through to the end. Just as he was winding up his speech, with the judge seeming to be fairly sympathetic to the lawyer's argument, the defendant ducked under the arm of his guard and made a dash for freedom! He had not got past the front steps of the courthouse before he was caught and brought back to the courtroom. The judge, understandably, raised the bail to quadruple what it had originally been.

Coining It In

A man in Arkansas who was arrested for a series of robberies from vending machines was taken to a preliminary hearing, where his bail was set at 300 dollars. The judge couldn't help but notice that he paid it all in quarters!

Close, But No Cigar

A man in America, having bought a case of forty very expensive Cuban cigars insured them, along with other valuable items in his possession, against theft, damage and fire. A couple of months later, having smoked all of them, the man filed an insurance claim for their loss in several instances of 'small fires'! The insurance company, understandably, refused to pay up, and so the man took them to court. The judge explained that while this was one of the most bizarre cases he had judged, the insurance company had not specified what kind of fire the cigars were being insured against, and that they should therefore pay up.

The insurance company later got their revenge, however, when they prosecuted the man for forty cases of arson!

Catch A Cold

After having shot a police officer during a raid on his house, a man made a run for it into nearby woods. After a long chase in freezing cold winter weather, the man contracted a mild case of hypothermia. He later tried to sue the police for not having done their job quickly enough and thus causing him to develop the condition! The case was, not surprisingly, thrown out of court.

Bigmouth Strikes Again

The trial of a young man from Liverpool for the armed robbery of a garage was going well for him, until the garage attendant testified that the young man was indeed the thief. Upon hearing this, the defendant leapt to his feet and yelled angrily, 'That's a lie! I wish I'd shot you while I had the chance!' Realizing his mistake, the man then falteringly added, 'If it had been me there, I mean.' With this, his defence fell apart, and the judge took very little time to find him guilty, recommending a particularly long jail sentence.

Your House Should Be More Burglar-Friendly!

A man who had just robbed a large sprawling mansion in Beverly Hills decided it was safest to exit via the garage at the back. However, he was not able to open the garage door as it was jammed and the automatic control was broken. When he tried to re-enter the house, he found that the door had locked when he pulled it shut behind him. He knew from watching the house for several weeks beforehand that the owners had gone on holiday, but had no way of knowing when they were due back. The only sustenance he had was a large bottle of mineral water and tins of dog food which he managed to eke out until the family returned ten days later. He then sued the family's insurance company for the physical and mental stress he had endured. He won the case and was awarded nearly a quarter of a million dollars in compensation!

The Stupidest
Drug
CRIMINALS

Drugs seem to addle the
brains of stupid criminals
and make them even more
prone to do something
seriously dumb ...

Nervous Criminal

A man returning from a holiday in Amsterdam was trying to smuggle a small amount of marijuana back into Britain. He was of a very nervous disposition, and the air stewardesses had noticed him sweating profusely and mumbling away to himself on the plane. When the time came for him to pick his luggage up off the carousel before proceeding through customs his nerve finally broke and he grabbed the nearest suitcase off the carousel. When the customs officer saw the man's sweating white face he became suspicious and asked to search his luggage. The man, now very glad that he had not picked up his own suitcase, congratulated himself on what a close call he had had, and agreed to the search. When the officer opened up the stranger's suitcase he found a large quantity of heroin stashed in one of the pockets!

Borderline Case

A group of criminals trying to smuggle a large amount of cocaine over the Dutch border hired a large truck and decorated it to look like the delivery van of a well-known food supplier. They hadn't been paying enough attention, however, and managed to misspell the name of the company – a mistake promptly investigated by custom officials.

Bad Customer Service

A man accosted a policeman on the street and showed him a bag of speed. He told him that it had been cut with other substances and demanded that the dealer he had purchased it from be arrested and forced to refund his money. Appearing to agree, the policeman allowed the man to take him back to the dealer, whereupon he immediately arrested the pair of them.

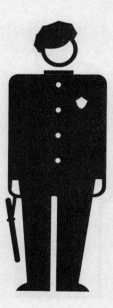

Pull the Other One

A suspected drug dealer in Quebec was arrested, and the police went round to his house that same afternoon. They found over twenty thousand pounds in cash stashed under the floorboards. The reason the dealer's mother gave for having such a large amount of cash was that she was saving up to buy a prosthetic leg for her son. The police were not fooled for a second by this excuse – the boy had spent much of the morning running away from them on two perfectly sound legs!

Return to Sender

A teenager in California hit upon the idea of sending his friend in England a small amount of cocaine via recorded post. Unsurprisingly, police dogs sniffed out the drugs in the package and the police had no problem finding the boy as he had put his name and address in the return to sender section on the envelope!

Call the cops

A young man in Illinois had been smoking one of his joints in the garden shed where he grew marijuana but had not extinguished it properly. When the shed caught alight, he had to call the fire brigade in – who, in turn, called the cops.

A Right Charlie

Two criminals on a housebreaking job thought they had hit the jackpot when, as well as the usual valuables, they found a pot on the mantelpiece labelled 'Charlie'. Being big cocaine takers, they snorted it there and then before carrying on with their theft. However, what the pair didn't realize was that 'Charlie' was actually the ashes of the homeowners' dead pet dog who had been cremated a couple of days earlier! After that experience, the twosome never touched drugs again.

Don't Call Again

Two young men on holiday in South America got chatting to a man in a bar who gave them the telephone number of his friend, telling them to call should they want to buy any cocaine. Later on in the week, the pair decided to call the dealer, although the man's writing was difficult to decipher and the number was not very clear. The person on the other end of the telephone told them that they had the wrong number and hung up. The two men, thinking they had perhaps misunderstood as neither spoke the local language very well, called back and repeated their request to buy cocaine. Unfortunately, the number they were ringing was the mobile telephone number of a police officer who, in the second conversation, pretended to be the drug dealer and arranged a meeting. When the men turned up at the appointed time they were promptly arrested.

The Stupidest Ill-Equipped CRIMINALS

As the following stories demonstrate, all too often it's the little things in life that matter. The stupid criminal is plagued by guns that won't fire, taxi-drivers that spill the beans and demand notes that identify the robber. Some days, nothing seems to go right.

Hot Money

A gang of men hijacked a train carrying over a million pounds in a safe. Overpowering the guards, they rigged up the safe with dynamite and waited in the adjoining carriage for the door of the safe to be blown open. They had used a particularly explosive form of dynamite, however, and the force of the explosion not only separated the part of the train that the men were in from that that the money was in, it also set light to the carriage containing the safe, reducing most of the money to a pile of ashes.

Let's Do A Deal

A gang of criminals kidnapped a wealthy young man in Morocco and demanded a hefty ransom from his father. Unfortunately for the kidnappers, while his father was putting together the money the young man managed to escape and returned home. The gang obviously didn't know when they were beaten, however, and then demanded a greatly reduced sum to defray the expenses of the abduction. The boy's father agreed, and arranged to meet them in a deserted parking lot to hand over the money. The criminals turned up at the designated place, at the right time to be greeted not with a wad of cash as they had expected, but the police!

You've Been Framed

A brave young man, who happened to be queuing in a bank when a robber burst in, made an attempt to tackle him. Unfortunately, he was easily overpowered by the armed criminal but, during the tussle, the robber's mask slipped off. Realizing that the bank's security camera would be recording the entire incident he pulled it off its stand and made his getaway with it and the loot, thinking he had successfully made off with all the evidence. What he hadn't realised was that, like most security cameras, the videotape itself was in the back office, recording remotely.

Accidental Crime

A man on a busy underground train on his way to work felt himself suddenly being jostled as the train braked unexpectedly. Feeling in his trouser pocket he realized his wallet had gone missing. Furious, he turned to the young man who had fallen against him and demanded, 'Give me the wallet!' The man stared at him in shock but handed over the wallet before hurriedly getting off at the next stop.

When the man arrived at work, however, he found a message from his wife telling him that he had left his wallet at home. He had to go to the police station and sheepishly hand the wallet in!

Take Note

Many thieves make bad decisions when it comes to choosing the writing material on which to write their ransom demands. One of the worst culprits was a thief in Oklahoma who walked into a clothes store and presented a note demanding the day's takings. The cashier obeyed and the man grabbed his loot and fled, leaving the note on the counter. When the cashier flipped it over she found it was actually the criminal's parole card – he had only been out of prison for only a few days. It wasn't long before he was back behind bars again.

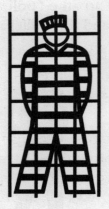

Cheque It Out!

Another criminal who made a particularly bad choice of writing material turned up at an exclusive London restaurant. The waitress was most taken aback when, after enjoying a three course meal, the man paid his bill with a cheque which had a message written on the back: 'I am armed, and will shoot unless you bring me all the money in the till'. The waitress did as instructed, and the man left, apparently believing that his hold-up had been a success.

Of course, as soon as he had gone the waitress called the police and supplied them with all his bank details. With this information the police had no problem arresting the man and recovering all the money – in addition, the restaurant cashed the hefty cheque covering the price of the meal and a generous tip for the waitress.

Taken For A Ride

A young man who did not own a car called a taxi to drive him to the bank he was intending to rob and wait outside while he carried out the heist. Several of the bank's staff and customers saw him step into the cab outside to make his getaway. It was therefore a simple job to contact the taxi firm and ask the driver where the man had been picked up and dropped off – his home address!

Slip Up

A man who tried to rob a fast food restaurant using a hand grenade gave the game away when he slipped on the recently washed floor and flung it across the restaurant. As the grenade did not at this point go off, his threat to set if off unless the cashier handed over all the money in the till seemed rather hollow. The man was forced to beat a hasty retreat amid the howls of laughter of both the staff and the customers.

Stuck In The Mud

A man fleeing from police after having attacked his wife's lover got stuck in the mud as he tried to run into nearby woods. In his hurry, he left the boots behind and carried on running. Police eventually tracked him down in the toilets of a fast food restaurant, wrapping toilet paper round his cold feet!

Plumb Crazy!

A man who broke into an empty house to steal jewellery and cash was caught when a neighbour spotted his van driving away. The van was the man's own and was clearly marked with the name of the man's dishwasher repair company. The neighbour later said she was suspicious of the van because she knew her neighbours did not even have a dishwasher!

Dirty Work

Two French criminals thought they were going the right way about robbing a mobile phone store when they put socks on their hands to avoid leaving fingerprints behind. Although their plan was essentially a sound one, their standards of hygiene could have

been better. Instead of using a couple of clean pairs, the socks they chose to use for the job were so badly in need of a wash that police dogs were able to track them down within the hour, just from the smell!

Russian Roulette

A man in Russia walked into a gun store and tried to hold up the owner with a six-inch knife. The owner and his assistant – perhaps unsurprisingly – both instantly pulled their guns on the man. His knife proved rather ineffective when faced with two handguns.

Poor Handiwork

A young woman who did not have a gun nevertheless decided to hold up a post office. She thought holding out her finger and thumb would fool the assistant into thinking she was armed. Perhaps it would have done if she had remembered to keep her hand in the pocket of her jacket!

Freeze!

An elderly man attempting to steal a frozen turkey from a supermarket for his Christmas lunch chose an unusual place to hide it – he tucked under his hat. His theft went undetected but the effect of the frozen bird, combined with the cold winter weather, caused him to develop a mild case of hypothermia. He had managed to stagger barely a few yards from the store before collapsing. A nearby policeman came to his assistance, and soon discovered the man's ailment – and crime – when he removed his hat.

Unusual Getaway

A man who robbed all seventy of his fellow passengers on board an internal flight in Australia turned out to be less capable at needlecraft than he at first thought. He used a parachute that he had made himself out of old sheets to make his escape, but the fabric soon came apart in mid-air. Miraculously, he survived, but the police were waiting to arrest him as soon as he regained consciousness.

Lock In

Two thieves left their car engine running outside while they were robbing a post office in order to make the speediest possible getaway. When they came outside, however, they found that the car battery had run out.

Custom-made Belt

It is illegal and can be dangerous to smuggle endangered creatures into Great Britain but that didn't stop our stupid criminal from Hull. While on holiday in

South America, the lady bought a rare breed of python on the black market and decided to bring it home with her. Instead of hiding the snake in her luggage or secreting it about her person she adopted the theory that guilt is best hidden in plain view. She gave the reptile a sedative and put it through the loops on her trouser waistband, trying to pass it off as a belt. It's unlikely but she might possibly have got away with it if it hadn't been for the fact that the snake woke up as she was going through custom checks and began to move around.

Trouser Snakes

A female customs officer was alarmed when she noticed a bulge moving in the trousers of a man who had just returned from from Africa. Embarrassed, she nevertheless asked the man to undress so she could investigate further. The man obeyed, only to reveal several baby snakes, stuffed in socks in his underpants, that he had been trying to illegally smuggle into the country.

Other Michael O'Mara Humour titles available:

The World's Stupidest Laws – ISBN 978-1-84317-172-0 pb £4.99
The World's Stupidest Signs – ISBN 978-1-84317-170-6 pb £4.99
More of the World's Stupidest Signs – ISBN 978-1-84317-032-7 pb £4.99
World's Stupidest Last Words – ISBN 978-1-84317-021-1 pb £4.99
The World's Stupidest Criminals – ISBN 978-1-84317-171-3 pb £4.99
The World's Stupidest Headlines – ISBN 978-1-84317-105-8 pb £4.99
The World's Stupidest Instructions – ISBN 978-1-84317-078-5 pb £4.99
The World's Stupidest Sporting Screw-Ups – ISBN 978-1-84317-039-6 pb £4.99
The World's Stupidest Chat-up lines – ISBN 978-1-84317-019-8 ISBN pb £4.99
The World's Stupidest Husbands – ISBN 978-1-84317-168-3 pb £4.99
The World's Stupidest Celebrities – ISBN 978-1-84317-137-9 pb £4.99
The World's Stupidest Deaths – ISBN 978-1-84317-136-2 pb £4.99

These titles and all other Michael O'Mara titles are available by post from:
Bookpost Ltd.,
PO Box 29,
Douglas,
Isle of Man,
IM99 1BQ

Credit cards accepted.
Telephone: 01624 677237
Fax: 01624 670923
Email: bookshop@enterprise.net
Internet: www.bookpost.co.uk

Free postage and packing in the UK.